Romeo and Juliet

The Shorter Shakespeare

Adapted from William Shakespeare

By Tracy Irish

Contents

Cover photograph: Royal Exchange Theatre, Manchester (This photograph survived the IRA bomb in 1996, which severely damaged the theatre, closing it for two years.)
Shakespeare portrait: By courtesy of the National Portrait Gallery, London
Title page photograph: National Youth Theatre of Great Britain. Photographer: Stuart Colwill

Published by Carel Press Ltd, 4 Hewson Street, Carlisle, Tel 01228 538928
info@shortershakespeare.com
www.shortershakespeare.com
www.carelpress.com

© Tracy Irish and Carel Press 1999
Reprinted 2001
Consultant: Jonathan Morris, English Adviser for South Tyneside
All rights are reserved. No part of this book may be reproduced or transmitted, in any form or by any means, without permission.

For permission to give a public performance of this play please write to Carel Press. (No fee will be charged for a performance in a school or youth club unless an admission charge is made, however, permission is still required.)

Printed by MFP Manchester on 100% recycled paper.

CIP Data: A catalogue record for this book is available from The British Library.

ISBN 1 872365 54 X

INTRODUCTION

The particular beauty of Romeo and Juliet, and its lasting appeal, is its vision of pure love. We can be cynical and dismissive in our modern age about the circumstances of Romeo and Juliet's love, but we cannot help having a sneaking admiration for and envy of such passion.

The play is written about young people and has much to interest them – not just the portrayal of the joys and heartache of first love and sexual attraction, but also the issues of rebellion against parents and believing oneself to be misunderstood.

So if the play has so much to offer, why do we need a shortened version? Well, even as someone who loves Shakespeare and is familiar with the language, I sometimes find myself 'switching off' whilst reading the long speeches or those comic lines, full of contemporary references, which just aren't funny today (unless you see a very good live performance).

This is not to say that Shakespeare wrote too much. Any close study at advanced level shows how important all the words are, just as a good professional performance needs the full text to explore all the nuances of character. But we have to appreciate that not everyone is ready to cope with reading a long play in what sometimes seems like a foreign language. Many students need an introduction to Shakespeare that will engage them in the story, interest them in the characters and introduce them to the language. Hackneyed as the phrase, 'making Shakespeare accessible' may now be, that is still our priority for each new group of students.

The idea of this script, then, is to show the essence of Romeo and Juliet, hinting at the further complexities that await more advanced study, but making the text manageable and accessible, for everyone.

On some occasions the order of the action has been changed. Notably, the second half of Act 1 Scene 2 has been moved to Act 1 Scene 1; in Act 3, Scene 4 has been switched with the first half of Scene 5; in Act 5, all the action takes place in Scene 1, at the Capulet Tomb. This rearrangement avoids some very short scenes, but continues the action and maintains the dramatic tension of the original.

The chorus is used to fill in the gaps in the action where cuts have been made. Details of changed scenes are given in the Teacher's Resource Book, where some of the cut sections are available for detailed study and annotation.

This shortened version was designed with two purposes in mind: to be studied and to be performed.

A shortened version of Romeo and Juliet was originally a project to introduce young children to Shakespeare through performance by secondary students to children in local primary schools. The objective was not just to show the story, but also to engender an enjoyment of the language. The result also proved popular with older and adult audiences.

My original aims were to produce a play that students would enjoy performing and a wide audience would appreciate. I believe that this script can fulfil these aims for other teachers and that the accompanying Teacher's Resource Book will enhance enjoyment and appreciation for those studying in the classroom.

Tracy Irish

Character List

The Montague Family and Friends

Lord Montague, Lady Montague

Romeo
Their son. At the start of the play, Romeo is in love with Rosaline

Mercutio
Romeo's friend. Mercutio is related to Prince Escalus

Benvolio
Romeo's cousin as well as his friend

Abraham & Balthasar
Servants of the Montagues

The Capulet Family and Friends

Lord Capulet, Lady Capulet

Juliet
Their daughter

Tybalt
Juliet's cousin

The Nurse
Who has looked after Juliet since she was a baby

Paris
A young nobleman who wants to marry Juliet.
He is related to Prince Escalus

Sampson, Gregory & Servant
Servants of the Capulets

Others

Prince Escalus
Ruler of Verona

Friar Lawrence
A priest who ministers to both the Montagues and the Capulets

Chorus 1   Chorus 2   Chorus 3   Crowd

*The role of the chorus has been divided between three separate speakers. Generally, Chorus 1 is a neutral narrator, Chorus 2 tends to look at the realities of the situation, while Chorus 3 has a more romantic viewpoint. The modern speeches of the chorus are printed in a different typeface.

Setting the Scene

Chorus 1: If you have ever been to the town of Verona in Italy, you may have been to a small courtyard, overlooked by an old stone balcony. If you have, you will have seen a golden statue of a young girl, Juliet Capulet.

Chorus 2: Juliet was the beautiful daughter of Lord and Lady Capulet, a distinguished and wealthy family who lived in Verona in the Middle Ages. Juliet's closest friend was the Nurse who had looked after her since her birth. Tybalt was her proud, ill-tempered cousin.

Chorus 1: The Capulets were the sworn enemies of another wealthy, distinguished family of the town, the Montagues.

Chorus 3: Romeo was the only son of Lord and Lady Montague. Benvolio was his cousin and friend. Mercutio, though not a Montague, was also a close friend.

Chorus 1: That golden statue of Juliet celebrates one of the most famous stories in the world, and is about one of the greatest themes of all time – how love can conquer hate.[1]

Chester Gateway Theatre
Photographer: Geoff Wilding

[1] History records that in the thirteenth century, a wealthy family from Verona called 'Montecchi' were involved in a feud with a family called 'Capelleti'. No other details are recorded but the story of Romeo and Juliet grew from some seeds of truth, into the play we know today.

The Prologue

Chorus 1:   Two households, both alike in dignity,
In fair Verona, where we lay our scene,
From ancient grudge break to new mutiny,
Where civil blood makes civil hands unclean.

Chorus 2:   From forth the fatal loins of these two foes
A pair of star-crossed lovers take their life,
Whose misadventured piteous overthrows
Doth with their death bury their parents' strife.

Chorus 3:   The fearful passage of their death-marked love,
And the continuance of their parents' rage,
Which, but for their children's end, nought could remove,
Is now the two hours' traffic of our stage;

Chorus 1:   The which if you with patient ears attend,
What here shall miss, our toil shall strive to mend.

The Royal Exchange Theatre Company, Manchester
Photographer: Stephen Vaughan

Act 1 Scene 1

Verona's Streets

Two Capulet servants, Gregory and Sampson, are talking in the street. Two Montague servants, Abraham and Balthasar, come by.

Gregory: Here comes two of the house of the Montagues.

Sampson: Quarrel; I will back thee.

Gregory: How? Turn thy back and run?

Sampson: Fear me not.

Gregory: I will frown as they pass by and let them take it as they list.

Sampson: Nay as they dare. I will bite my thumb at them which is disgrace to them if they bear it.

Sampson aims this insulting gesture at the Montague servants who cannot ignore it.

Abraham: Do you bite your thumb at us, sir?

Sampson: I do bite my thumb, sir.

Abraham: Do you bite your thumb at us, sir?

Gregory: Do you quarrel, sir?

Abraham: Quarrel, sir? No, sir.

Sampson: But if you do, sir, I am for you. I serve as good a man as you. Draw if you be men.

A fight breaks out. Benvolio and Tybalt enter from opposite directions.

Benvolio: Part fools!
Put up your swords; you know not what you do.

Tybalt approaches Benvolio, who speaks to him

I do but keep the peace: put up thy sword.

7

Tybalt: Peace? I hate the word,
As I hate hell, all Montagues and thee.
Have at thee, coward.

Other Montagues and Capulets join the fight as crowds gather to watch.
Lord and Lady Capulet enter.

Lord Capulet: What noise is this? Give me my long sword, ho!

Lady Capulet: A crutch, a crutch! Why call you for a sword?

Lord Capulet: My sword, I say! Old Montague is come,
And flourishes his blade in spite of me.

Lord and Lady Montague enter.

Lord Montague: Thou villain Capulet! – Hold me not, let me go.

Lady Montague: Thou shalt not stir one foot to seek a foe.

Prince Escalus enters and the crowds part to let the Prince through.

Prince: Rebellious subjects, enemies to peace.
Will they not hear? What ho! You men! You beasts!
On pain of torture, from those bloody hands
Throw your mistempered weapons to the ground,
And hear the sentence of your moved prince.

The fighting stops.

Three civil brawls, bred of an airy word
By thee, old Capulet, and Montague,
Have thrice disturbed the quiet of our streets.
If ever you disturb our streets again
Your lives shall pay the forfeit of the peace.
For this time, all the rest depart away.
You, Capulet, shall go along with me;
And, Montague, come you this afternoon.
Once more, on pain of death, all men depart.

All but Lord and Lady Montague and Benvolio leave.

Lord Montague: Who set this ancient quarrel new abroach?

Benvolio: Here were two servants of your adversary
And yours, close fighting ere I did approach:
I drew to part them; in the instant came
The fiery Tybalt, with his sword prepared.
While we were interchanging thrusts and blows
Came more and more, and fought on part and part,
Till the Prince came, who parted either part.

Lady Montague: O where is Romeo? Saw you him today?
Right glad I am, he was not at this fray.

Benvolio: Madam, early did I see your son;
Towards him I made, but he was ware of me,
And stole into the covert of the wood.

Lord Montague: Many a morning hath he there been seen,
With tears augmenting the fresh morning's dew.

Benvolio: My noble uncle, do you know the cause?

Lord Montague: I neither know it, nor can learn of him.
Could we but learn from whence his sorrows grow,
We would as willingly give cure as know.

Romeo approaches.

Benvolio: See where he comes! So please you, step aside;
I'll know his grievance or be much denied.

Lord Montague: I would thou wert so happy by thy stay
To hear true shrift[2]. Come, madam, let's away.

Lord and Lady Montague depart.

Benvolio: Good morrow cousin.

Romeo: O me! What fray was here?
Yet tell me not, for I have heard it all:
Here's much to do with hate, but more with love.

Romeo and Benvolio continue to talk quietly.

---

[2] Confession.

Chorus 1:   Romeo could see there had been a fight and could guess what it had all been about.

Chorus 2:   He's seen it all before and knows all about the fierce loyalty and love each family has for its own – and how much hatred this breeds against the other family.

Chorus 1:   Of course, Romeo loves his family too, but he is preoccupied by a different love – his love for a girl called Rosaline. That is the cause of the recent strange behaviour that has puzzled his family and friends.

Chorus 3:   He has been busy writing poems and songs for Rosaline. He is desperately in love with her ...

Chorus 2:   But she has no interest in him.

Romeo: Love is a smoke made with the fume of sighs,
Being purged, a fire sparkling in lovers' eyes;
Being vexed, a sea nourished with lovers' tears.
What is it else? A madness most discreet,
A choking gall,[3] and a preserving sweet.

Benvolio: Be ruled by me; forget to think of her.

Romeo: O, teach me how I should forget to think.

Benvolio: By giving liberty unto thine eyes;
Examine other beauties.
Take thou some new infection to thy eye,
And the rank poison of the old will die.

They are interrupted by a Capulet servant who needs some help.

Servant: I pray you, sir, can you read?

Romeo: Ay, if I know the letters and the language.

Servant: Ye say honestly: rest you merry.

The servant begins to leave.

Romeo: Stay, fellow; I can read.

---

[3]   A bitter poison.

Romeo reads aloud from the servant's sheet.

> "Signior Martino and his wife and daughters,
> County Anselmo and his beauteous sisters,
> Mercutio and his brother, Valentine,
> My fair niece Rosaline and Livia,
> Lucio and the lively Helena,"
> A fair assembly: whither should they come?

Servant: To supper; to our house.

Romeo: Whose house?

Servant: My master's. My master is the great rich Capulet;
and if you be not of the house of Montagues, I pray
come and crush a cup of wine. Rest you merry.

The servant departs.

Benvolio: At this same ancient feast of Capulet's
Sups the fair Rosaline whom thou so loves,
With all the admired beauties of Verona:
Go thither, and with unattainted eye
Compare her face with some that I shall show,
And I will make thee think thy swan a crow.

Romeo: One fairer than my love! The all-seeing sun
Ne'er saw her match since first the world begun.

They depart still talking.

Act 1 Scene 2

Introduction

Chorus 2: Here in the Capulet household, everyone is busy with arrangements for the party, but Juliet's father also has another important issue to consider.

Chorus 3: An offer of marriage for his daughter from a wealthy and well connected young man called Paris.

Chorus 1: It's quite usual for parents to arrange marriages for their daughters – and for girls to be married young.

Act 1 Scene 2

The Capulet House

Enter Lord Capulet and Paris, talking.

Lord Capulet: But Montague is bound as well as I,
In penalty alike; and 'tis not hard, I think,
For men so old as we to keep the peace.

Paris: Of honourable reckoning are you both,
And pity 'tis you lived at odds so long.
But now, my lord, what say you to my suit?

Lord Capulet: But saying o'er what I have said before:
My child is yet a stranger in the world;
She hath not seen the change of fourteen years;
Let two more summers wither in their pride
Ere we may think her ripe to be a bride.

Paris: Younger than she are happy mothers made.

Lord Capulet: And too soon marred are those so early made.
But woo her, gentle Paris, get her heart;
My will to her consent is but a part.
This night I hold an old accustomed feast,

Whereto I have invited many a guest,
Such as I love; and you among the store,
One more most welcome, makes my number more.

Lord Capulet and Paris depart.

Chorus 3: Will Juliet give her heart to Paris? He is considered rather good looking, as well as being rich and powerful.

Chorus 2: And well mannered and loyal ... she could do worse.

Act 1 Scene 3

Another room in the Capulet House

Enter Lady Capulet and the Nurse.

Nurse: What lamb! What lady-bird! God forbid, where's this girl? What Juliet?

Enter Juliet.

Juliet: How now, who calls?

Nurse: Your mother.

Juliet: Madam I am here. What is your will?

Lady Capulet: This is the matter. Nurse, give leave a while:
We must talk in secret. Nurse, come back again:
I have remembered me; thou s'hear our counsel.
Thou knowest my daughter's of a pretty age.

Nurse: Faith, I can tell her age unto an hour.
On Lammas-Eve[4] at night shall she be fourteen.
That shall she, marry; I remember it well.
'Tis since the earthquake now eleven years,
And she was weaned – I never shall forget it –
Of all the days of the year upon that day.
My lord and you were then at Mantua.

---

[4] 31st July.

> And since that time it is eleven years.
> Thou wast the prettiest babe that e'er I nursed:
> An I might live to see thee married once,
> I have my wish.

Lady Capulet: Marry, that 'marry' is the very theme
I came to talk of. Tell me, daughter Juliet,
How stands your dispositions to be married?

Juliet: It is an honour that I dream not of.

Lady Capulet: Well think of marriage now; younger than you
Here in Verona, ladies of esteem,
Are made already mothers. By my count,
I was your mother much upon these years
That you are now a maid. Thus then in brief:
The valiant Paris seeks you for his love.

Nurse: A man, young lady! Lady, such a man
As all the world – Why, he's a man of wax[5].

Lady Capulet: Verona's summer hath not such a flower.

Nurse: Nay, he's a flower, in faith, a very flower.

Lady Capulet: What say you? Can you love the gentleman?
This night you shall behold him at our feast.

Juliet: I'll look to like if looking liking move.
But no more deep will I endart mine eye
Than your consent gives strength to make it fly.

Nurse: Go girl. Seek happy nights to happy days.

They all depart.

Chorus 1: So Juliet dutifully agrees to try to like Paris because
he is her parents' choice.

---

[5]   Perfect – as though modelled from wax.

Hull Truck Theatre Company
Photographer: Phil Cutts

Act 1 Scene 4

Verona's Streets

Enter Romeo, Benvolio, Mercutio and others, laughing and talking and carrying carnival masks.

Mercutio: Nay, gentle Romeo, we must have you dance.

Romeo: Not I, believe me: you have dancing shoes
With nimble soles; I have a soul of lead
So stakes me to the ground I cannot move.

Mercutio: You are a lover; borrow Cupid's wings,
And soar with them above a common bound.

Romeo: I am too sore enpierced with his shaft
To soar with his light feathers and so bound.
I cannot bound a pitch[6] above dull woe.
Under love's heavy burden do I sink.

---

[6]   The height at which a hawk hovers to look for prey. The whole of the exchange is full of puns.

Mercutio: And, to sink in it, should you burden love –
Too great oppression for a tender thing.

Romeo: Is love a tender thing? It is too rough,
Too rude, too boisterous, and it pricks like thorn.

Mercutio: If love be rough with you, be rough with love;
Prick love for pricking and you beat love down.
Give me a case to put my visage in.

Mercutio puts on his mask and plays the fool for his laughing companions.

Chorus 1: As a relative of Prince Escalus, Mercutio is on the guest list for the Capulet party, and, as all the guests will be wearing masks, Romeo and Benvolio can accompany Mercutio to the party without being recognised.

Chorus 2: Benvolio and Mercutio are hoping that a night out, drinking and dancing in the company of many beautiful women will make Romeo forget Rosaline.

Chorus 3: However, Romeo has doubts about the plan.

Romeo: And we mean well in going to this masque,
But 'tis no wit to go.

Mercutio: Why, may one ask?

Romeo: I dreamt a dream tonight.

Mercutio: And so did I.

Romeo: Well what was yours?

Mercutio: That dreamers often lie.

Romeo: In bed asleep, while they do dream things true.

Mercutio: O then I see Queen Mab[7] hath been with you.

Benvolio: Supper is done, and we shall come too late.

Romeo: I fear, too early, for my mind misgives
Some consequence, yet hanging in the stars,

---

[7] Queen of the fairies, she affects the dreams of mortals. (The full speech appears in the accompanying Teacher's Resource Book.)

Shall bitterly begin his fearful date
With this night's revels, and expire the term
Of a despised life closed in my breast,
By some vile forfeit of untimely death.
But He that hath the steerage of my course
Direct my sail! On, lusty gentlemen.

*They make their way to the Capulet house, putting on
their masks as they go.*

Chorus 3:   Romeo has misgivings about attending the party –
but he doesn't want to let his friends down, and he
still hopes to see Rosaline there.

Act 1 Scene 5
The Capulet House

Chorus 1: The Capulet party is a grand affair with plenty of food and drink. Juliet is introduced to Paris ... and Lord Capulet welcomes his guests, including Mercutio and his disguised friends.

Lord Capulet: You are welcome, gentlemen! Come musicians, play.
A hall, a hall. Give room, and foot it, girls!

The dancing and festivities begin. While the guests dance, Romeo looks about for Rosaline and notices Juliet.

Romeo: What lady's that which doth enrich the hand
Of yonder knight?
O, she doth teach the torches to burn bright!
Did my heart love till now? Forswear it, sight!
For I ne'er saw true beauty till this night.

Tybalt, walking past, hears Romeo's last lines.

Tybalt: This by his voice should be a Montague.
(To a servant) Fetch me my rapier, boy.
Now, by the stock and honour of my kin,
To strike him dead I hold it not a sin.

Lord Capulet: Why, how now, kinsman! Wherefore storm you so?

Tybalt: Uncle, this is a Montague, our foe.

Lord Capulet: Young Romeo is it?

Tybalt: 'Tis he, that villain, Romeo.

Lord Capulet: Content thee, gentle coz, let him alone.
'A bears him like a portly gentleman;
And to say the truth, Verona brags of him
To be a virtuous and well governed youth.
I would not for the wealth of all this town
Here in my house do him disparagement.

---

[8] A palmer was a pilgrim.

Hull Truck Theatre Company
Photographer: Phil Cutts

> Show a fair presence and put off these frowns,
> An ill-beseeming semblance for a feast.

Tybalt: It fits when such a villain is a guest:
I'll not endure him.

Lord Capulet: He shall be endured.
Go to, go to! You are a saucy boy!

They move back to the party.

Romeo gains Juliet's attention and quietly leads her aside.

Romeo: If I profane with my unworthiest hand,
This holy shrine, the gentle sin is this:
My lips, two blushing pilgrims ready stand
To smooth that rough touch with a tender kiss.

Juliet: Good pilgrim, you do wrong your hand too much
Which mannerly devotion shows in this;
For saints have hands that pilgrims' hands do touch
And palm to palm is holy palmers'[8] kiss.

Romeo: Have not saints lips and holy palmers too?

Juliet: Ay, pilgrim, lips that they must use in prayer.

Romeo: O then, dear saint, let lips do what hands do:
They pray: grant thou, lest faith turn to despair.

Juliet: Saints do not move, though grant for prayers' sake.

Romeo: Then move not, while my prayer's effect I take.
Thus from my lips, by thine, my sin is purged.

They kiss.

Juliet: Then have my lips the sin that they have took.

Romeo: Sin from my lips? O trespass sweetly urged!
Give me my sin again.

He kisses her again

Juliet: You kiss by th' book.

The Nurse approaches.

Royal Shakespeare Company
Photographer: Ivan Kyncl

21

Nurse: Madam, your mother craves a word with you.

Juliet takes her leave of Romeo.

Romeo: What is her mother?

Nurse: Marry, bachelor,
Her mother is the lady of the house,
I nursed her daughter that you talked withal.

The Nurse goes to Juliet.

Romeo: Is she a Capulet?
O dear account! My life is my foe's debt.

The party breaks up and goodbyes are said.

Juliet: What's he that follows there, that would not dance?

Nurse: I know not

Juliet: Go, ask his name.

The Nurse does so.

          – If he be married,
My grave is like to be my wedding bed.

Nurse: His name is Romeo, and a Montague,
The only son of your great enemy.

Juliet: My only love sprung from my only hate!
Too early seen unknown, and known too late!

Nurse: Come, let's away; the strangers all are gone.

All depart.

22

Act 2
Introduction

Chorus 3:   So Romeo's old love for Rosaline is now dead. Her beauty cannot match Juliet's.

Chorus 2:   And Romeo's good looks have likewise charmed Juliet. But their love is difficult and dangerous and must be kept secret.

Chorus 1:   Romeo cannot openly visit the house of his enemy and Juliet is not allowed out without a very good reason.

Chorus 2:   How will they meet again?

Chorus 3:   Well, love will find a way.

Act 2 Scene 1
Outside the Capulet House

Benvolio and Mercutio are looking for Romeo.

Benvolio: Romeo! My cousin, Romeo! Romeo!
He ran this way and leapt this orchard wall.
Call, good Mercutio.

Mercutio: Nay, I'll conjure too[9].
Romeo! Humours! Madman! Passion! Lover!

Benvolio: Come! He hath hid himself among these trees.

Mercutio: Come, shall we go?

Benvolio: Go then, for 'tis in vain
To seek him here that means not to be found.

Romeo emerges from his hiding place.

Romeo: He jests at scars that never felt a wound.

---

[9]   A pun on conjuring up a spirit or a devil, which can allegedly be summoned when the right name is spoken.

Chorus 3: Romeo knows his friends don't understand his feelings of love because they have never been in love themselves.

Chorus 1: He sets off in search of his new love. He scales the garden wall of the Capulet house and looks for Juliet's bedroom window.

Chorus 2: This is dangerous territory for a Montague. If any of Juliet's relatives find him, Romeo is in deep trouble.

Act 2 Scene 2

The Capulet Orchard

Juliet appears on her balcony.

Romeo: But soft, what light through yonder window breaks?
It is the east, and Juliet is the sun!
Arise, fair sun, and kill the envious moon,
Who is already sick and pale with grief,
That thou, her maid, art far more fair than she.
It is my lady, O, it is my love!
O that she knew she were!

Juliet: Ay me!

Romeo: She speaks.

Juliet: Oh Romeo, Romeo, wherefore art thou Romeo?
Deny thy father and refuse thy name.
Or if thou wilt not, be but sworn my love,
And I'll no longer be a Capulet.
'Tis but thy name that is my enemy.
What's in a name? That which we call a rose
By any other name would smell as sweet;
So Romeo would were he not Romeo called,
Retain that dear perfection which he owes
Without that title. Romeo, doff thy name;
And for thy name, which is no part of thee,
Take all myself.

Romeo comes forward.

Romeo: I take thee at thy word.
Call me but love, and I'll be new baptised;
Henceforth I never will be Romeo.
My name, dear saint, is hateful to myself,
Because it is an enemy to thee.

Juliet: My ears have not yet drunk a hundred words
Of thy tongue's uttering, yet I know the sound.
Art thou not Romeo and a Montague?

Romeo: Neither, fair maid, if either thee dislike.

Juliet: How cam'st thou hither, tell me, and wherefore?
The orchard walls are high and hard to climb
And the place death, considering who thou art,
If any of my kinsmen find thee here.

Romeo: With love's light wings did I o'erperch these walls,
For stony limits cannot hold love out,
And what love can do, that dares love attempt;
Therefore thy kinsmen are no stop to me.

Juliet: I would not for the world they saw thee here.

Romeo: I have night's cloak to hide me from their eyes,
And but thou love me, let them find me here;
My life were better ended by their hate
Than death prorogued,[10] wanting of thy love.

Juliet: Thou knowest the mask of night is on my face,
Else would a maiden blush bepaint my cheek
For that which thou hast heard me speak tonight.
Dost thou love me? I know thou wilt say 'Ay!',
And I will take thy word. Yet if thou swear'st,
Thou mayst prove false. At lovers' perjuries,
They say Jove laughs. O gentle Romeo,
If thou dost love, pronounce it faithfully.
Or if thou think'st I am too quickly won,
I'll frown and be perverse and say thee nay,

---

[10] Postponed, put off.

> So thou wilt woo; but else, not for the world.
> In truth, fair Montague, I am too fond,
> And therefore thou mayst think my 'haviour light;
> But trust me, gentleman, I'll prove more true
> Than those that have more cunning to be strange.

Romeo: Lady, by yonder blessed moon I vow,
That tips with silver all these fruit tree tops –

Juliet: O swear not by the moon, th'inconstant moon,
That monthly changes in her circled orb,
Lest that thy love prove likewise variable.

Romeo: What shall I swear by?

Juliet: Do not swear at all:
Or, if thou wilt, swear by thy gracious self,
Which is the god of my idolatry,
And I'll believe thee.

Romeo: If my heart's dear love –

Juliet: Well, do not swear. Although I joy in thee,
I have no joy of this contract tonight:
It is too rash, too unadvised, too sudden,
Too like the lightning, which doth cease to be
Ere one can say 'It lightens'. Sweet, goodnight:
This bud of love, by summer's ripening breath,
May prove a beauteous flower when next we meet.
Goodnight, goodnight! As sweet repose and rest
Come to thy heart as that within my breast.

Romeo: O wilt thou leave me so unsatisfied?

Juliet: What satisfaction canst thou have tonight?

Romeo: Th'exchange of thy love's faithful vow for mine.

Juliet: I gave thee mine before thou didst request it:
I hear some noise within. Dear love, adieu –

The Nurse calls.

> Anon, good nurse! – sweet Montague, be true.
> If that thy bent of love be honourable,
> Thy purpose marriage, send me word tomorrow.

Nurse: *(calling from within)* Madam!

Romeo: So thrive my soul –

Juliet: A thousand times good night!

Juliet goes in.

Romeo: A thousand times the worse, to want thy light!

Juliet returns.

Juliet: 'Tis almost morning. What o'clock tomorrow
Shall I send to thee?

Romeo: By the hour of nine.

Juliet: I will not fail. 'Tis twenty year till then.
Goodnight, goodnight. Parting is such sweet sorrow
That I shall say goodnight till it be morrow.

Romeo: Sleep dwell upon thine eyes, peace in thy breast.
Would I were sleep and peace so sweet to rest.

Juliet goes in and Romeo departs.

Chorus 1: So Romeo's capacity for love has met its match in Juliet.

Chorus 2: He has forgotten Rosaline and Juliet has forgotten her promise to her parents to marry Paris. Both are prepared to pursue their love in spite of the trouble between their families.

Chorus 3: Like Romeo, Juliet lets her heart rule her head. All their thoughts are now whirling around the idea of marriage and the consummation of their love.

Chorus 1: Romeo goes immediately to see his priest and friend, Friar Lawrence.

Act 2 Scene 3

Outside Friar Lawrence's Cell at Dawn

Enter Friar, picking herbs. Romeo approaches.

Romeo: Good morrow, father.

Friar: Benedicite!
What early tongue so sweet saluteth me?
Thou art uproused with some distemperature;
Or if not so, then here I hit it right –
Our Romeo hath not been in bed tonight.

Romeo: That last is true – the sweeter rest was mine.

Friar: God pardon sin! Wast thou with Rosaline?

Romeo: With Rosaline? My ghostly father, no.
I have forgot that name, and that name's woe.

Friar: That's my good son! But where hast thou been then?

Romeo: I'll tell thee ere thou ask it me again:
I have been feasting with mine enemy.

Romeo and the Friar continue talking quietly.

Chorus 1: Romeo tells Friar Lawrence all about his new love, Juliet. The Friar is surprised at how quickly things have happened and wonders whether Romeo is simply in love with Juliet's looks.

Friar: Holy Saint Francis, what a change is here!
Is Rosaline, that thou didst love so dear,
So soon forsaken? Young men's love then lies
Not truly in their hearts, but in their eyes.

Chorus 3: But he agrees to marry the young lovers, hoping that such love between a Capulet and a Montague will end all the hatred and fighting.

Friar: But come, young waverer, come, go with me;
In one respect I'll thy assistant be:
For this alliance may so happy prove
To turn your households' rancour to pure love.

28

Romeo: O let us hence! I stand on sudden haste.

Friar: Wisely and slow; they stumble that run fast.

They depart.

Act 2 Scene 4

Friar Lawrence's Cell

Chorus 1: Later that morning, Juliet sends her Nurse to find Romeo. He sends a message back with the Nurse for Juliet to meet him and marry him at Friar Lawrence's chapel that afternoon.

Chorus 2: Visiting the Friar is a good reason for Juliet to leave the house. Her parents believe she has gone to confession!

Romeo and Juliet, accompanied by the Nurse, are married by Friar Lawrence.

Chorus 3: And so, Romeo and Juliet are secretly married by Friar Lawrence. The only other person who knows of the secret wedding is Juliet's doting nurse.

Crucible Theatre, Sheffield

Act 3 Scene 1

Introduction

Chorus 3:　Romeo and Juliet could not be happier.

Chorus 1:　They care nothing for the fight between their families and believe that nothing but good can happen now. But Tybalt, Juliet's cousin...

Chorus 3:　And Romeo's cousin too, now!

Chorus 1:　Yes, and Romeo's cousin too, now that Romeo and Juliet are married. Tybalt has not forgotten that Romeo gatecrashed the Capulets' party and he is determined to get revenge.

Chorus 3:　But Romeo is in such a good mood after his wedding that he loves everyone, even Tybalt.

Chorus 2:　It's a shame not everyone shares his good mood on this hot, sultry, Italian afternoon. Tybalt is angry – and Mercutio is irritable – perhaps because of the hot weather; perhaps because of his friend's recent secrecy.

Act 3 Scene 1

Verona's Streets

Benvolio and Mercutio are talking in the streets.

Benvolio:　I pray thee good Mercutio, let's retire.
　　　　　　　The day is hot and the Capels[11] are abroad
　　　　　　　And if we meet, we shall not 'scape a brawl.
　　　　　　　For now, these hot days is the mad blood stirring.

Tybalt enters with friends.

　　　　　　　By my head here comes the Capulets.

Mercutio:　By my heel I care not.

---

[11]　A shortened version of 'Capulets'.

Tybalt: Gentlemen, a word with one of you.

Mercutio: And but one word with one of us? Couple it with something; make it a word and a blow.

Tybalt: Mercutio, thou consortest with Romeo –

Mercutio: Consort? What, dost thou make us minstrels?[12] An thou make minstrels of us, look to hear nothing but discords.

He draws his sword and jabs at Tybalt's feet to make him jump back.

   Here's my fiddlestick; here's that shall make you dance. Zounds! Consort!

Benvolio: We talk here in the public haunt of men.
Either withdraw unto some private place,
Or reason coldly of your grievances,
Or else depart. Here all eyes gaze on us.

Mercutio: Men's eyes were made to look, and let them gaze.
I will not budge for no man's pleasure, I.

Romeo approaches.

Tybalt: Well peace be with you, sir; here comes my man.
Romeo, the love I bear thee can afford
No better term than this: thou art a villain.

Romeo: Tybalt, the reason that I have to love thee
Doth much excuse the appertaining rage
To such a greeting. Villain am I none –
But love thee better than thou canst devise
Till thou shalt know the reason of my love:
And so, good Capulet, which name I tender
As dearly as mine own, be satisfied.

---

[12]   Tybalt uses the word consort to mean 'keep company with' but consort is also a term for a group of hired musicians, such as minstrels. Mercutio deliberately takes the word as an insult because minstrels were of a low class.

National Youth Theatre of Great Britain
Photographer: Stuart Colwill

Mercutio: O calm, dishonourable, vile submission!
Tybalt you rat catcher,[13] will you walk?

Mercutio draws his sword.

Tybalt: What wouldst thou have with me?

Mercutio: Good King of Cats, nothing but one of your nine lives.

Tybalt: I am for you.

Tybalt draws his sword and they fight.
Romeo tries to stop them.

Romeo: Gentle Mercutio, put thy rapier up.
Gentlemen, for shame, forbear this outrage.
Tybalt, Mercutio, the Prince expressly hath
Forbid this bandying in Verona streets.
Hold Tybalt. Good Mercutio.

As Romeo gets between them, Tybalt stabs Mercutio, then backs away and leaves.

Mercutio: I am hurt!
A plague on both your houses. I am sped.

Benvolio: What, art thou hurt?

Mercutio: Ay, ay, a scratch, a scratch; marry tis enough.

Romeo: Courage, man, the hurt cannot be much.

Mercutio: No, 'tis not so deep as a well, nor so wide as a church door, but 'tis enough, 'twill serve. Ask for me tomorrow and you shall find me a grave man. A plague on both your houses! Why the devil came you between us? I was hurt under your arm.

Romeo: I thought all for the best.

Mercutio: A plague o' both your houses!
They have made worms' meat of me.
Your houses!

Mercutio falls. Benvolio goes to him.

---

[13] The name Tybalt is similar to the name of the cat in a medieval story of Reynard the Fox – the name we know as Tibbles.

Benvolio: O Romeo, Romeo, brave Mercutio's dead.

Romeo: This day's black fate on moe days doth depend,
This but begins the woe others must end.

Benvolio: Here comes the furious Tybalt back again.

Romeo: Again, in triumph, and Mercutio slain!

Tybalt returns.

Now Tybalt, take the 'villain' back again
That late thou gavest me, for Mercutio's soul
Is but a little way above our heads
Staying for thine to keep him company.
Either thou, or I, or both must go with him.

Tybalt: Thou wretched boy, that didst consort him here,
Shalt with him hence.

Romeo: This shall determine that.

They fight and Romeo kills Tybalt.

Benvolio: Stand not amazed. The Prince will doom thee death
If thou art taken. Hence, be gone, away!

Romeo: O, I am Fortune's fool.

Benvolio: Why dost thou stay?

Romeo turns and runs away.
Crowds gather. The Prince, Lord and Lady Capulet and
Lord and Lady Montague arrive. Lady Capulet weeps
over the body of Tybalt.

Prince: Where are the vile beginners of this fray?

Benvolio: O, noble Prince, I can discover all
The unlucky manage of this fatal brawl.
There lies the man, slain by young Romeo,
That slew thy kinsman brave Mercutio.

Lady Capulet: Tybalt, my cousin![14] Prince as thou art true,
For blood of ours shed blood of Montague.

---

[14] Cousin is a general term for a relative or 'kinsman'. Tybalt is Lady Capulet's nephew.

The Prince draws Benvolio aside.

Prince: Benvolio, who began this bloody fray?

Benvolio: Tybalt, here slain, whom Romeo's hand did slay.

They continue to talk quietly.

Chorus 1: Benvolio tells the Prince everything that happened.

Chorus 2: Except how Mercutio had provoked Tybalt.

Chorus 3: Benvolio explains how Romeo had tried to keep the peace' – refusing to fight with Tybalt himself and trying to stop the fight between Tybalt and Mercutio; but when Tybalt killed his best friend, Romeo's temper had snapped.

Chorus 1: It is clear that Tybalt began the fight and the Prince has some sympathy for Romeo's actions. But two men still lie dead and the Prince represents the law in Verona. He cannot just pardon Romeo.

The Prince and Benvolio return to the crowd.

Lady Capulet: I beg for justice, which thou, Prince, must give.
Romeo slew Tybalt. Romeo must not live.

Prince: Romeo slew him, he slew Mercutio.
Who now the price of his dear blood doth owe?

Lord Montague: Not Romeo, Prince, he was Mercutio's friend;
His fault concludes but what the law should end,
The life of Tybalt.

Prince: And for that offence
Immediately we do exile him hence.
Else when he is found, that hour is his last.

All depart.

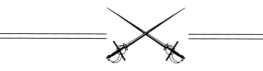

Act 3 Scene 2

Juliet's Bedroom

Juliet sits alone.

Chorus 3: Unaware of all these tragic events, Juliet is waiting impatiently for night to fall, so that her Romeo can climb up to her window and the newly wedded couple can be together.

Juliet: Gallop apace, you fiery-footed steeds,
Towards Phoebus' lodging![15] Such a waggoner
As Phaeton would whip you to the west
And bring in cloudy night immediately.[16]
Come gentle night; come, loving, black-browed night;
Give me my Romeo; and, when he shall die,
Take him and cut him out in little stars,
And he will make the face of heaven so fine
That all the world will be in love with night,
And pay no worship to the garish sun.
O, I have bought the mansion of a love
But not possess'd it, and though I am sold,
Not yet enjoy'd. So tedious is this day.

Enter the Nurse, clearly distressed.

Ay me, what news? Why dost thou wring thy hands?

Nurse: Ah well-a-day! He's dead, he's dead, he's dead!
We are undone, lady, we are undone.

Juliet: Can heaven be so envious?

Nurse: Romeo can.
Though heaven cannnot. O Romeo, Romeo!
Who ever would have thought it? Romeo!

---

[15] Phoebus is another name for the Greek sun god.
[16] Phaeton is the son of the sun god in Greek legend. He borrowed his father's chariot of the sun, but couldn't control the horses. Zeus struck him dead with a thunderbolt in case he burned up the earth. An ironic story for Juliet to mention.

Juliet: What devil art thou that dost torment me thus?
This torture should be roared in dismal hell.
Hath Romeo slain himself? Say thou but 'Ay'
And that bare vowel 'I' shall poison more
Than the death-darting eye of cockatrice.[17]

Nurse: I saw the wound, I saw it with mine eyes,
(God save the mark!) here on his manly breast.
A piteous corse, a bloody piteous corse,
Pale, pale as ashes, all bedaubed in blood,
All in gore blood; I swooned at the sight.

Juliet: O break, my heart! Poor bankrupt,[18] break at once!

Nurse: O Tybalt, Tybalt, the best friend I had!
That ever I should live to see thee dead!

Juliet: What storm is this that blows so contrary?
Is Romeo slaughtered; and is Tybalt dead?
My dearest cousin, and my dearer lord?

Nurse: Tybalt is gone and Romeo banished;
Romeo that killed him, he is banished.

Juliet: O God! Did Romeo's hand shed Tybalt's blood?

Nurse: It did, it did! Alas the day, it did!

Juliet: O serpent heart, hid with a flowering face!
Beautiful tyrant, fiend angelical,
A damned saint, an honourable villain!
Was ever book containing such vile matter
So fairly bound? O that deceit should dwell
In such a gorgeous palace.

Nurse: There's no trust,
No faith, no honesty in men; all perjured,
All forsworn, all naught, all dissemblers.
Shame come to Romeo!

Juliet: Blistered be thy tongue
For such a wish! He was not born to shame.

---

[17] A legendary monster, half cockerel, half snake, that could kill with a glance.
[18] Bankrupt meaning at the end of one's resources, exhausted.

Chester Gateway Theatre
Photographer: Geoff Wilding

Nurse: Will you speak well of him that killed your cousin?

Juliet: Shall I speak ill of him that is my husband?
But wherefore, villain, didst thou kill my cousin?
That villain cousin would have killed my husband.
My husband lives, that Tybalt would have slain,
And Tybalt's dead that would have slain my husband;
All this is comfort; wherefore weep I then?
'Tybalt is dead and Romeo banished'.
'Romeo is banished'! To speak that word
Is father, mother, Tybalt. Romeo, Juliet,
All slain, all dead: 'Romeo is banished'!

She picks up a rope ladder which had been prepared for Romeo to climb up to her window.

Take up those cords. Poor ropes, you are beguiled,
Both you and I, for Romeo is exiled.
He made you for a highway to my bed,
But I, a maid, die maiden-widowed.
Come cords; come, Nurse: I'll to my wedding bed,
And death, not Romeo, take my maidenhead!

Nurse: Hie to your chamber. I'll find Romeo
To comfort you: I wot well where he is.

Juliet: O find him! Give this ring to my true knight
And bid him come to take his last farewell.

The Nurse takes the ring and quickly leaves.

Act 3 Scene 3

Friar Lawrence's Cell

The Friar and Romeo are talking animatedly.

Chorus 1: Romeo has run to Friar Lawrence, devastated by all that has happened.

Friar: Hence from Verona art thou banished
Be patient, for the world is broad and wide.

Romeo: There is no world without Verona walls,
But purgatory, torture, hell itself.

Friar: O deadly sin, O rude unthankfulness.
Thy fault our law calls death, but the kind Prince,
Taking thy part, hath rush'd aside the law
And turn'd that black word 'death' to banishment.
This is dear mercy and thou seest it not.

Romeo: Tis torture and not mercy. Heaven is here
Where Juliet lives, and every cat and dog
And little mouse, every unworthy thing,
Live here in heaven and may look on her,
But Romeo may not, he is banished.
O Friar, the damned use that word in hell.

Friar: Thou fond mad man, hear me a little speak.

Romeo: Thou canst not speak of that thou dost not feel.
Wert thou as young as I, Juliet thy love,
An hour but married, Tybalt murdered,
Doting like me, and like me banished,
Then mightest thou speak, then mightest thou
tear thy hair,
And fall upon the ground as I do now,
Taking the measure of an unmade grave.

Romeo falls to the ground and weeps.
The Nurse enters.

Nurse: O holy Friar, O tell me holy Friar,
Where is my lady's lord? Where's Romeo?

Friar: There on the ground, with his own tears made drunk.

Nurse: Piteous predicament. Even so lies she,
Blubbering and weeping, weeping and blubbering.
(To Romeo) Stand up, stand up. Stand, and you be
a man.
For Juliet's sake, for her sake, rise and stand.

Romeo: Spakest thou of Juliet? How is it with her?
Doth she not think me an old murderer,
Now I have stained the childhood of our joy
With blood removed but little from her own?
How doth she? O, tell me, Friar, tell me,
In what vile part of this anatomy
Doth my name lodge? Tell me, that I may sack
The hateful mansion[19].

Romeo is about to stab himself.

Friar: Hold thy desperate hand!
Art thou a man? Thy form cries out thou art.
Thy tears are womanish, thy wild acts denote
The unreasonable fury of a beast.
What, rouse thee, man! Thy Juliet is alive,
For whose dear sake thou wast but lately dead.
There art thou happy. Tybalt would kill thee,
But thou slewest Tybalt. There art thou happy.
The law that threatened death becomes thy friend,
And turns it to exile. There art thou happy.
A pack of blessings light upon thy back.
Happiness courts thee in her best array;
But like a mishav'd and a sullen wench
Thou pouts upon thy fortune and thy love.
Go get thee to thy love, as was decreed;
Ascend her chamber; hence and comfort her.
But look thou stay not till the Watch be set,
For then thou canst not pass to Mantua,
Where thou shalt live till we can find a time
To blaze your marriage, reconcile your friends,
Beg pardon of the Prince, and call thee back.
Go before Nurse. Commend me to thy lady.

---

[19]   An echo of Juliet's descriptions of Romeo as the 'mansion of a love' and as a 'gorgeous palace' hiding deceit.

Nurse:　*(to Romeo)* My lord, I'll tell my lady you will come.

Romeo:　Do so, and bid my sweet prepare to chide.

The Nurse makes to leave, then turns back.

Nurse:　Here, sir, a ring she bid me give you, sir.
Hie you, make haste, for it grows very late.

Romeo takes the ring.

Romeo:　How well my comfort is revived by this.

Act 3 Scene 4
Juliet's Bedroom

Romeo and Juliet lie asleep in her bed.

Chorus 1:　So, Romeo must leave Verona to lie low in the nearby town of Mantua. He can only hope that soon he may be able to return.

Chorus 3:　Before Romeo leaves Verona, he has come to the Capulets' house in secret to spend his first and last night with his new wife. Juliet understands why Romeo killed her hot-tempered cousin and forgives him. Her only concern now is for the passionate but fragile love they share.

Chorus 2:　They both know that Tybalt's death has made things even more difficult for them.

Romeo wakes and begins to rise from the bed.

Juliet:　Wilt thou be gone? It is not yet near day.
It was the nightingale, and not the lark,
That pierced the fearful hollow of thine ear.
Believe me, love, it was the nightingale.

Romeo:　It was the lark, the herald of the morn,
No nightingale. Look, love, what envious streaks
Do lace the severing clouds in yonder east.
I must be gone and live, or stay and die.

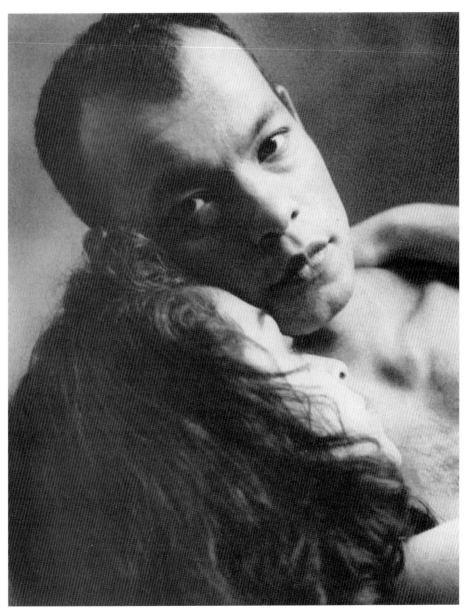

Hull Truck Theatre Company
Photographer: Phil Cutts

Juliet: Yond light is not daylight, I know it, I.
          Therefore stay yet: thou need'st not to be gone.

Romeo: Let me be ta'en, let me be put to death,
          I am content, so thou wilt have it so.
          I have more care to stay than will to go.
          Come death, and welcome. Juliet wills it so.
          How is't, my soul? Let's talk. It is not day.

Juliet: It is, it is! Hie hence, be gone, away!
          It is the lark that sings so out of tune,
          Straining harsh discords and unpleasing sharps.
          O now be gone, more light and light it grows.

Romeo: More light and light; more dark and dark our
          woes.

The Nurse enters.

Nurse: Madam!

Juliet: Nurse?

Nurse: The day is broke; be wary, look about.

The Nurse leaves.

Juliet: Then, window, let day in and let life out.

Romeo: Farewell, farewell, one kiss and I'll descend.

Juliet: Art thou gone so? Love, lord, ay husband, friend.

Romeo begins to climb down from Juliet's window.

          O, think'st thou we shall ever meet again?

Romeo: I doubt it not; and all these woes shall serve
          For sweet discourses in our times to come.

Juliet: O God, I have an ill-divining soul!
          Methinks I see thee, now thou art so low,
          As one dead in the bottom of a tomb.
          Either my eyesight fails or thou look'st pale.

Romeo: And trust me, love, in my eye so do you.
          Dry sorrow drinks our blood. Adieu, adieu!

Act 3 Scene 5

The Capulet House

Enter Lord and Lady Capulet and Paris, talking.

Chorus 1: Juliet's parents are, of course, unaware of her marriage to Romeo and believe all her tears are for Tybalt.

Chorus 2: Despite the very recent death of their nephew, they are still preparing for her marriage to Paris.

Lord Capulet: Things have fall'n out, sir, so unluckily
That we have had no time to move our daughter.
Look you, she loved her kinsman Tybalt dearly,
And so did I. Well, we were born to die.

Paris: These times of woe afford no times to woo.

Lord Capulet: Sir Paris, I will make a desperate tender
Of my child's love: I think she will be ruled
In all respects by me: nay more, I doubt it not.
O'Thursday let it be –

(to his wife)   O'Thursday, tell her,
She shall be married to this noble earl –

(to Paris) Will you be ready? Do you like this haste?

Paris: My lord, I would that Thursday were tomorrow.

Lord Capulet: Well, get you gone. O'Thursday be it then.
Prepare her, wife, against this wedding day.

They all depart.

Act 3 Scene 6

Juliet's bedroom

Juliet is weeping for the loss of Romeo. Her mother enters.

Chorus 2: This is the last thing Juliet will want to hear.

Lady Capulet: Why, how now, Juliet?

Juliet: Madam, I am not well.

Lady Capulet: Ever more weeping for your cousin's death?
We will have vengeance for it, fear thou not.
Then weep no more. That villain, Romeo!
But now I'll tell thee joyful tidings girl.
Marry, my child, early next Thursday morn
The gallant young and noble gentleman
The County Paris, at St Peter's Church
Shall happily make thee there a joyful bride.

Juliet: Now by St Peter's Church and Peter too
He shall not make me there a joyful bride.
I wonder at this haste, that I must wed
Ere he that should be husband comes to woo.
I pray you tell my lord and father, madam,
I will not marry yet; and when I do, I swear
It shall be Romeo, whom you know I hate,
Rather than Paris. These are news indeed!

Lady Capulet: Here comes your father, tell him so yourself.

Lord Capulet: What, girl, still in tears? How now, wife?
Have you delivered to her our decree?

Lady Capulet: Ay sir, but she will none, she gives you thanks
I would the fool were married to her grave!

Lord Capulet: How? Will she none? Doth she not give us thanks?
Is she not proud? Doth she not count her blest,
Unworthy as she is, that we have wrought
So worthy a gentleman to be her bride?

Juliet: Not proud that you have, but thankful that you have.
Proud can I never be of what I hate,
But thankful even for hate that is meant love.

Lord Capulet: How now! how now, chop-logic! What is this?
'Proud', and 'I thank you', and 'I thank you not',
And yet 'not proud', mistress minion you?
Thank me no thankings nor proud me no prouds,
But fettle your fine joints against Thursday next
To go with Paris to St Peter's Church
Or I will drag thee on a hurdle thither.
Out, you green sickness carrion! Out you baggage!
You tallow face!

Lady Capulet: *(to her husband)* Fie, fie! what are you mad?

Juliet: Good father, I beseech you on my knees,
Hear me with patience but to speak a word.

Lord Capulet: Hang thee young baggage! Disobedient wretch!
I'll tell thee what; get thee to church o' Thursday
Or never after look me in the face.
Speak not, reply not, do not answer me!
My fingers itch.

Nurse: God in heaven bless her!
You are to blame, my lord, to rate her so.

Lord Capulet: And why, my Lady Wisdom? Hold your tongue.

Nurse: May not one speak?

Lord Capulet: Peace, you mumbling fool!
Utter your gravity o'er a gossip's bowl,[20]
For here we need it not.

Lady Capulet: You are too hot.

Lord Capulet: God's bread! It makes me mad! Day, night, work, play,
Alone, in company, still my care hath been
To have her matched; and having now provided
A gentleman of noble parentage,
Stuffed, as they say, with honourable parts,

---

[20] Tell your opinions to the other gossips.

And then to have a wretched puling fool,
To answer, 'I'll not wed, I cannot love;
I am too young; I pray you pardon me'.
But an you will not wed, I'll pardon you –
Graze where you will; you shall not house with me.
Thursday is near. Lay hand on heart; advise.
An you be mine, I'll give you to my friend;
An you be not, hang, beg, starve, die in the streets,
For by my soul I'll ne'er acknowledge thee.

Lord Capulet leaves.

Juliet: Is there no pity sitting in the clouds
That sees into the bottom of my grief?
O sweet mother, cast me not away!
Delay this marriage for a month, a week;
Or, if you do not, make the bridal bed
In that dim monument where Tybalt lies.

Lady Capulet: Talk not to me, for I'll not speak a word.
Do as thou wilt for I have done with thee.

Lady Capulet leaves.

Juliet: O God, O Nurse, how shall this be prevented?
My husband is on earth, my faith in heaven.
What sayst thou? Hast not a word of joy?
Some comfort, Nurse.

Nurse: Faith, here it is.
I think it best you married with the County.
O, he's a lovely gentleman!
Romeo's a dishclout[21] to him. An eagle, madam,
Hath not so green, so quick, so fair an eye
As Paris hath. Beshrew my very heart,
I think you are happy in this second match,
For it excels your first; or, if it did not,
Your first is dead, or 'twere as good he were
As living here and you no use of him.

Juliet: Speakest thou from thy heart?

---

[21] A dishcloth – limp and weak.

Nurse: And from my soul too, else beshrew them both.

Nurse kisses Juliet and leaves.

Juliet: Ancient damnation! O most wicked fiend.
Thou and my bosom henceforth shall be twain.

Juliet dresses herself, while she considers what to do.

Chorus 2:   Poor Juliet. Her parents won't listen to her or give
her any choice about marrying Paris. Her father, at
first reluctant himself to see her married so young ...

Chorus 3:   Or to someone she didn't love ...

Chorus 2:   ... Now threatens to disown her and throw her out
into the streets if she doesn't obey him. Her mother
will not help her and nor will her Nurse.

Chorus 3:   Juliet feels betrayed and very alone.

Juliet: I'll to the Friar to know his remedy.
If all else fail, myself have power to die.

National Youth Theatre of Great Britain
Photographer: Stuart Colwill

Act 4 Scene 1

Friar Lawrence's Cell

Enter the Friar and Paris, talking.

Chorus 1: Paris, believing that Juliet is willing to marry him, is making arrangements with the Friar.

Chorus 2: The Friar knows only too well just how complicated the situation is becoming and how much trouble it could bring if the truth comes out now – for the lovers and for himself.

Friar: On Thursday, sir? The time is very short.

Paris: My father Capulet will have it so,
And I am nothing slow to slack his haste.

Friar: You say you do not know the lady's mind?
Uneven is the course; I like it not.

Paris: Immoderately she weeps for Tybalt's death.

Friar: Look, sir, here comes the lady toward my cell.

Juliet approaches.

Paris: Happily met, my lady and my wife!

Juliet: That may be, sir, when I may be a wife.

Paris: That 'may be' must be, love, on Thursday next.

Juliet: What must be shall be.

Friar: That's a certain text.

Paris: God shield I should disturb devotion!
Juliet, on Thursday early will I rouse ye;
Till then, adieu, and keep this holy kiss.

He kisses her, then leaves.

Juliet: O shut the door, and, when thou hast done so,
Come weep with me – past hope, past cure, past help.
If in thy wisdom thou canst give no help,
Do thou but call my resolution wise
And with this knife I'll help it presently.

O bid me leap, rather than marry Paris,
From off the battlements of any tower,
Or walk in thievish ways, or bid me lurk
Where serpents are; chain me with roaring bears,
Or bid me go into a new made grave
And hide me with a dead man in his shroud,
And I will do it without fear or doubt,
To live an unstained wife to my sweet love.

The Friar comforts Juliet, then talks to her quietly.

Chorus 3: Juliet is willing to suffer any torment rather than marry Paris and be unfaithful to Romeo.

Chorus 2: Her words are very brave and so obviously sincere that the Friar decides to take a chance on a dangerous plan that has occurred to him – that they should simulate Juliet's death, using a powerful drug.

Friar: Hold, then. Go home, be merry, give consent
To marry Paris. Wednesday is tomorrow.
Tomorrow night look that thou lie alone.
Take thou this vial, being then in bed,
And this distilled liquor drink thou off.
No warmth, no breath, shall testify thou livest.
And in this borrowed likeness of shrunk death
Thou shalt continue two and forty hours,
And then awake as from a pleasant sleep.

The Friar and Juliet continue to talk, then pray together.

Chorus 1: The Friar promises to send a message to Romeo in Mantua to tell him of the plan. Everyone will think Juliet is dead and take her to the family tomb in the local graveyard. When she wakes up, exactly forty two hours after drinking the potion, Romeo will be at her side and the two of them can leave Verona together.

Juliet and the Friar rise from their prayers.

Juliet: Love give me strength, and strength shall help afford.
Farewell, dear father.

Juliet leaves.

Act 4 Scene 2

The Capulet House

Enter Lord and Lady Capulet and the Nurse. Juliet follows.

Lord Capulet: How now, my headstrong? Where have you been gadding?

Juliet: Where I have learned me to repent the sin
Of disobedient opposition
To you and your behests, and am enjoined
By holy Lawrence to fall prostrate here
To beg your pardon. Pardon, I beseech you!
Henceforward I am ever ruled by you.

Juliet kneels.

Lord Capulet: Why, I am glad on't. This is well. Stand up.
(To servant) Send for the County, go tell him of this.
I'll have this knot knit up tomorrow morning.

Lady Capulet: No, not till Thursday. There is time enough.

Lord Capulet: Go, Nurse, go with her; we'll to church tomorrow.

The Nurse departs with Juliet.

Lady Capulet: We shall be short in our provision,
'Tis now near night.

Lord Capulet: Tush I will stir about,
And all things shall be well, I warrant thee, wife.
Go thou to Juliet; help to deck up her.
Let me alone; my heart is wondrous light
Since this same wayward girl is so reclaimed.

They depart.

Act 4 Scene 3

Juliet's Bedroom

Juliet and the Nurse are laying out clothes for the wedding.
Lady Capulet enters.

Lady Capulet: What, are you busy, ho? Need you my help?

Juliet: So please you, let me now be left alone,
And let the Nurse this night sit up with you,
For I am sure you have your hands full all
In this so sudden business.

Lady Capulet: Good night.
Get thee to bed and rest, for thou hast need.

Lady Capulet and the Nurse leave.

Juliet: Farewell! God knows when we shall meet again.
I have a faint cold fear thrills through my veins.
I'll call them back again to comfort me.
– Nurse! – What should she do here?
My dismal scene I needs must act alone.
Come vial!
What if this mixture do not work at all?
Shall I be married then tomorrow morning?
No, no! This shall forbid it. Lie thou there.

She lays her dagger beside her.

What if it be poison which the Friar
Subtly hath minist'red to have me dead,
Lest in this marriage he should be dishonoured
Because he married me before to Romeo?
I fear it is; and yet methinks it should not,
For he hath still been tried a holy man.
How if, when I am laid into the tomb,
I wake before the time that Romeo
Come to redeem me? There's a fearful point!
Shall I not then be stifled in the vault,
To whose foul mouth no healthsome air breathes in?

53

Or, if I live, is it not very like,
The horrible conceit of death and night,
Together with the terror of the place –
Where for this many hundred years the bones
Of all my buried ancestors are packed,
Where bloody Tybalt lies festering in his shroud,
O, if I wake, shall I not be distraught,
Environed.with all these hideous fears,
And madly play with my forefathers' joints?

Chorus 1:　Juliet is terrified of what may await her – but her choices are limited. She is alone with her fears.

Chorus 3:　Her love for Romeo gives her courage.

Juliet:　Romeo, Romeo, Romeo, here's drink! I drink to thee!

Juliet drinks the potion and falls on her bed.

Hull Truck Theatre Company
Photographer: Phil Cutts

Act 4 Scene 4

Juliet's Bedroom

Juliet lies on her bed. The Nurse enters and begins to draw the curtains.

Chorus 1: The next morning, as the Capulet household stirs, on the day that Juliet is supposed to marry Paris, the Nurse comes to Juliet's bedroom to wake her.

Nurse: Why, lamb! Why, lady! Fie, you slug-a-bed!
Why, love, I say! Madam! Sweetheart! Why, bride!
Sleep for a week; for the next night I warrant,
The County Paris hath set up his rest
That you shall rest but little. God forgive me!
I must needs wake you. Lady, lady, lady!

The Nurse shakes Juliet.

Alas, alas! Help! Help! My lady's dead!

Lady Capulet rushes in.

Lady Capulet: What is the matter?

Nurse: Look, look! O heavy day.

Lady Capulet goes to her daughter.

Lady Capulet: O me, O me! My child, my only life!
Revive, look up, or I will die with thee.

Enter Lord Capulet.

Lord Capulet: For shame, bring Juliet forth, her lord is come.

Nurse: She's dead, deceas'd! She's dead! Alack the day!

Lady Capulet: Alack the day! She's dead, she's dead, she's dead!

Lord Capulet: Ha, let me see her. Out, alas! She's cold.

Nurse: O, lamentable day!

Lady Capulet: O, woeful time!

Chester Gateway Theatre
Photographer: Geoff Wilding

Enter Paris, Friar and others.

Friar: Come, is the bride ready to go to church?

Lord Capulet: Ready to go, but never to return.

Lady Capulet: Accurs'd, unhappy, wretched, hateful day.

Nurse: O woe! O woeful, woeful, woeful day!

Lord Capulet: *(To Paris)* O son, the night before thy wedding day
Hath Death lain with thy wife. There she lies,
Flower as she was, deflowered by him.
Death is my son-in-law, Death is my heir.

Paris: Beguiled, divorced, wronged, spited, slain!
Most detestable Death, by thee beguil'd.
O love! O life! Not life, but love in death!

Lord Capulet: O child, O child. My soul and not my child.
Dead art thou. Alack, my child is dead,
And with my child my joys are buried.

Friar: Peace, ho, for shame! Confusion's cure lives not
In these confusions. Heaven and yourself
Had part in this fair maid, now heaven hath all,
And all the better is it for the maid.
Dry up your tears and stick your rosemary
On this fair corse, and as the custom is,
All in her best array, bear her to church.

Juliet is taken to the tomb.

Act 5 Scene 1
Introduction

Chorus 2: So far, the Friar's plan seems to be working, but more misfortune is on the way. Romeo doesn't get the message from the Friar.

Chorus 1: The Friar's messenger stopped on his way to Mantua because people thought that he might have an infectious illness. He was not allowed to continue, nor would anyone take the message on for him in case the illness spread.

Chorus 2: Instead, Romeo hears Verona's news from his young servant, Balthasar. The boy has rushed to Mantua to tell Romeo that Juliet is dead.

Chorus 3: Romeo visits a poor apothecary, from whom he buys poison. Then rides fast back to Verona to be with Juliet.

Act 5 Scene 1
The Capulet Tomb

Juliet and Tybalt lie in the tomb. Paris sits by the gates.

Chorus 1: While Romeo is riding back to Verona, poor Paris is grieving for the girl who nearly became his wife. He sits quietly by the tomb.

Paris: Sweet flower, with flowers thy bridal bed I strew.
O woe, thy canopy is dust and stones.
Which with sweet water nightly I will dew
Or wanting that with tears distilled by moans.
The obsequies[22] that I for thee will keep
Nightly shall be to strew thy grave and weep.

A whistle is heard.

The boy gives warning, something doth approach.
What cursed foot wanders this way tonight?

---
[22] Funeral rites.

Romeo enters and begins to break into the tomb.

Romeo: Thou detestable maw, thou womb of death,
Gorged with the dearest morsel of the earth,
Thus I enforce thy rotten jaws to open
And in despite I'll cram thee with more food.

Paris: This is that banished, haughty Montague
That murdered my love's cousin, with which grief
It is supposed the fair creature died
And here is come to do some villainous shame
To the dead bodies; I will apprehend him.
Stop thy unhallowed toil, vile Montague.

Romeo: Good, gentle youth, tempt not a desperate man.
Put not another sin upon my head
By urging me to fury. O be gone.

Paris: I do defy thy conjuration[23]
And apprehend thee for a felon here.

Romeo: Wilt thou provoke me? Then have at thee boy!

They fight and Romeo mortally wounds Paris.

Paris: O, I am slain. If thou be merciful
Open the tomb, lay me with Juliet.

Romeo: In faith, I will. Let me peruse this face.
Mercutio's kinsman, gentle County Paris!
What said my man when my betossed soul
Did not attend him as we rode? I think
He told me Paris should have married Juliet.
One writ with me in sour misfortune's book!

He drags the body into the tomb, then sees Juliet.

Here lies Juliet and her beauty makes
This vault a feasting presence full of light.
Death, that hath sucked the honey of thy breath,
Hath had no power yet upon thy beauty.
O, why art thou yet so fair? O, here

---

[23] A solemn entreaty.

> Will I set up my everlasting rest,
> And shake the yoke of inauspicious stars
> From this world wearied flesh. Eyes look your last!
> Arms, take your last embrace! And lips, O you,
> The doors of breath, seal with a righteous kiss
> A dateless bargain to engrossing Death!
> Here's to my love.

He drinks the poison.

> O, true apothecary!
> Thy drugs are quick. Thus with a kiss I die.

He kisses Juliet, then dies.

Chorus 3: The Friar comes to the tomb to meet Juliet when she awakes. He is hoping to keep her with him until he can send another message to Romeo.

The Friar rushes in.

Friar: Romeo! O, pale! Who else? What, Paris too?
And steeped in blood? Ah, what an unkind hour
Is guilty of this lamentable chance!
The lady stirs.

Juliet wakes.

Juliet: O comfortable Friar, where is my lord?
I do remember well where I should be,
And there I am. Where is Romeo?

Noises are heard.

Friar: A greater power than we can contradict
Hath thwarted our intents. Come, come away.
Thy husband in thy bosom there lies dead:
Stay not to question for the Watch is coming.
Come, go, good Juliet; I dare no longer stay.

Juliet: Go, get thee hence, for I will not away.

The Friar hesitates, then rushes away.

The Royal Exchange Theatre Company, Manchester
Photographer: Stephen Vaughan

What's here? A cup closed in my true love's hand?
Poison I see, hath been his timeless end.
O churl. Drunk all and left no friendly drop
To help me after? I will kiss thy lips,
Haply some poison yet doth hang on them
To make me die with a restorative.
Thy lips are warm.

More noises are heard. Juliet takes up Romeo's dagger.

Yea, noise? Then I'll be brief. O happy dagger
This is thy sheath. There rust, and let me die.

She stabs herself and falls on Romeo's body.
Enter Lord and Lady Capulet, the Prince, and others.
The Friar is brought in by a Watchman.

Chorus 1: Paris' servant has raised the alarm and brought everyone to the tomb.

Lord Capulet: O heavens! O wife, look how our daughter bleeds!

Enter Lord Montague.

Prince: Come, Montague, for thou art early up
To see thy son and heir now early down.

Lord Montague: Alas, my liege, my wife is dead tonight.
Grief of my son's exile hath stopp'd her breath.
What further woe conspires against mine age?

Prince: Look, and thou shalt see.

Lord Montague: O thou untaught! What manners is in this,
To press before thy father to a grave?

Prince: Bring forth the parties of suspicion.

The Friar steps forward.

Chorus 2: The Friar sadly explains everything – all about Romeo and Juliet's secret wedding; about the potion that Juliet took, and the fatal delay with the message that led to all their deaths.

Chorus 3: Both Romeo's family and Juliet's family realise how destructive their hatred and fighting has been.

Prince: Where be these enemies? Capulet? Montague?
See what a scourge is laid upon your hate
That heaven finds means to kill your joys with love.
And I for winking at your discords too
Have lost a brace of kinsmen. All are punished.

Lord Capulet: O brother, Montague, give me thy hand.

Lord Montague: But I can give thee more.
For I will raise her statue in pure gold.
That, whiles Verona by that name is known,
There shall no figure at such rate be set
As that of true and faithful Juliet.

Lord Capulet: As rich shall Romeo's by his lady's lie.
Poor sacrifices of our enmity!

Prince: A glooming peace this morning with it brings;
The sun for sorrow will not show his head.
Go hence, to have more talk of these sad things.
Some shall be pardoned, and some punished;
For never was a story of more woe
Than this of Juliet and her Romeo.

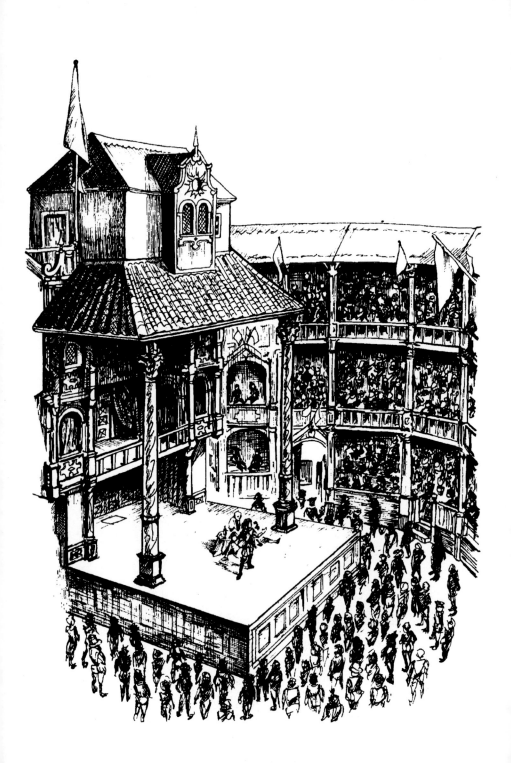